Baseball

Bernie Blackall

Heinemann Library
Des Plaines, Illinois

© 1999 Reed Educational & Professional Publishing
Published by Heinemann Library,
an imprint of Reed Educational & Professional Publishing
1350 East Touhy Avenue, Suite 240 West
Des Plaines, Illinois 60018

© Bernie Blackall 1999

03 02 01 00 99
10 9 8 7 6 5 4 3 2 1

All rights reserved. No part of this publication may be reproduced or transmitted in any form or by any means, electronic or mechanical, including photocopying, recording, taping, or any information storage and retrieval system, without permission in writing from the publisher.

Series cover and text design by Karen Young
Cover by Smarty-pants Design
Paged by Jo Pritchard
Edited by Jane Pearson
Illustrations by Joy Antonie
Picture research by Lara Artis
Production by Cindy Smith
Film separations by Typescan, Adelaide
Printed in Hong Kong by Wing King Tong

Library of Congress Cataloging-in-Publication Data

Blackall, Bernie, 1956-
    Baseball / Bernie Blackall.
       p.   cm. -- (Top sport)
    Includes bibliographical references (p.) and index.
    Summary: Introduces the history, skills, rules, equipment, and events of baseball.
    ISBN 1-57572-839-7 (library binding)
    1. Baseball -- Juvenile literature. [l. Baseball.] I. Title.
II. Series: Blackall, Bernie, 1956- Top sport.
GV867.5.B55 1999
796.357--dc21   98-43109
                                                                CIP
                                                                AC

Photographs supplied by: All Sport: (Stephen Dunn) p 7, (Vince Laforet) p 6. Australian Picture Library/ Corbis Bettmann: p 9. Bernie Blackall: pp 11 (right), 22 (left), 24 (right). Coo-ee Historical Picture Library: p 8. Sue and Wies Fajzullin Photography: cover, pp 12, 15, 16, 19 (top), 22 (right), 23, 24 (left). Liles Photography: cover, pp 4, 18, 25, 27. Barry Silkstone: pp 5, 10, 11 (left), 17, 19 (bottom), 20, 21, 26.

Every effort has been made to contact copyright holders of any material reproduced in this book. Any omissions will be rectified in subsequent printings if notice is given to the publisher.

Some words are shown in bold, **like this**. You can find out what they mean by looking in the glossary.

Contents

About Baseball	5
U.S Highlights	6
History of Baseball	8
What You Need to Play	10
Rules	14
Skills	18
Getting Ready	28
Taking it Further	*30*
More Books to Read	*30*
Glossary	*31*
Index	*32*

About Baseball

Baseball is a bat and ball game and is usually played between two teams of nine players. It is played in more than 75 countries and is the second most popular team sport in the world, behind soccer.

One team bats while the other team plays the field. The fielding team tries to stop the batting team from scoring runs by forcing "outs." The nine fielders play specific positions on the field. There is a pitcher, a catcher, a base fielder for first, second, and third bases, a shortstop, and three outfielders.

The batting team tries to score runs by advancing around the bases. A run is scored when a player on the batting team runs around the four bases in order without being forced out. A batter or runner usually doesn't complete the run on one hit. He or she is safe while on a base and can run from one base to the next each time the ball is pitched or even in between pitches if time-out has not been called. If a **base runner** is touched with the ball when off base, he or she is called out.

Each team takes turns batting and fielding. The turns are called **innings**. An inning lasts until both teams have batted and fielded once. A team's inning is completed when three players have been forced out. The winner is the team with the most runs after nine innings. Youth leagues often play games of seven innings.

Tee ball

Tee ball is a form of baseball for very young players. It involves hitting the ball off a stand called a **tee** rather than being pitched to by the fielding team.

The ball is pitched to the batter who hits it to run to base.

U.S. Highlights

Mark McGwire

Baseball is so popular in the United States that it is often called the "national pastime." Players from age six to adults play in organized leagues throughout the United States. No leagues are more popular than the professional Major Leagues: the National and American Leagues. Thousands of players have reached the Major Leagues, but only a few hundred have made a great impact on the game.

The Babe

No one has made a greater impact than Babe Ruth. From 1914 to 1935, Ruth hit 714 home runs. His larger-than-life personality and great talent made him the most popular player of the time and his New York Yankees famous around the world. Ruth's ability to hit towering home runs changed the way baseball was played. It also brought hundreds of thousands of fans to the stadiums, many of whom wanted to just see home runs.

Top Sport

Sammy Sosa

The Home Run

Nothing in baseball creates excitement or fan interest more than the home run. With one swing of the bat, a player can change a team's entire season. The interest Babe Ruth sparked with his home runs continues to this day. Ruth's all-time home run record of 714 stood for 39 years, until Hank Aaron hit his 715th in 1974. Aaron still holds the career record with 755 home runs.

Perhaps the most prized record in baseball has been the single-season home run mark, which Ruth broke in 1927 with 60. In 1961, Roger Maris, also of the New York Yankees, broke Ruth's record on the last day of the season to end with 61.

Mark and Sammy

In 1998, two players in the National League created just as much excitement as Ruth had in his magical 1927 season.

Mark McGwire of the St. Louis Cardinals and Sammy Sosa of the Chicago Cubs not only passed Ruth's mark, they bested Maris's 37-year-old record. Fans throughout the country flocked to the ballparks and their TV sets to follow the chase. On September 8, against Sosa's Chicago Cubs, McGwire hit his 62nd home run. McGwire finished the season with 70 to set a new Major League record.

Sosa also passed Roger Maris on his way to 66 home runs. The friendly home run competition between "Big Mac" and Sosa help draw fans back to the ballparks and inspired millions of young players with their talent and sportsmanship.

History of Baseball

Baseball developed from the English game of rounders. In 1829, Oliver Wendell Holmes organized a game of baseball at Harvard University after reading the rules of rounders. He is said to have modified the playing area into a diamond shape and to have adapted the "three-strike rule."

But it is also claimed that baseball began in Cooperstown, New York, in 1839. A West Point Army Cadet named Abner Doubleday is said to have laid out the first diamond-shaped field. Doubleday maintained that he invented the game without any knowledge of the English game rounders. Most historians have dismissed Doubleday's claims, however.

The modern game

Whatever its origins, there is no question that the game was established and refined to become the game it is today in the United States.

The modern game's first basic rules were developed by Alexander J. Cartwright in 1845. By 1858, 25 clubs formed the first baseball league in the U.S.: the National Association of Amateur Base Ball Players.

Spectators loved the game. It was not unusual as long ago as 1858 for 1,500 fans to pay 50 cents each to watch their favorite teams. The first professional team, the Cincinnati Red Stockings, was formed in 1869. In 1871, a professional league, the National Association of Professional Base Ball Players, was formed.

This illustration shows a baseball game in 1885. A batter slides into home plate.

The game of baseball was taken around the world by U.S. servicemen during the First and Second World Wars.

The World Series

In 1903, the existing two leagues were formed: the National League and the American League. The winner from each of these leagues meet in October each year to compete in the best of seven series, known as the World Series. This is one of the most popular sporting events in the U.S. Although it is not a true "world" competition, it is generally agreed that the competition in the U.S is the strongest in the world.

At the Olympics

After being a demonstration sport at the 1984 and 1988 Olympic Games, baseball is now a Competition Gold Medal Sport. The first medal competition was at the Barcelona Olympic Games in 1992.

What You Need to Play

The uniform

Each team wears uniforms with team colors and the team name on them. Uniforms should be close-fitting.

There are two kinds of baseball shoes: plastic spikes and metal **spikes.** Youth players wear shoes with molded plastic spikes on the soles. Leagues for older players allow the use of metal spikes. These give the best traction but can be dangerous for younger players.

Players wear caps in team colors to block out the sun while playing the field.

All **base runners** and batters must wear a protective helmet.

The catcher's gear

The catcher is well protected from fast pitches or **foul balls** off the bat. Catchers wear a mask as well as a helmet to protect the face and head. A throat protector can be attached to the mask. The chest protector covers the chest, stomach, and shoulders. Shin guards cover the knees and shins. A catcher's glove is flexible to permit one-handed catching, but also padded enough to provide protection for the fingers and hand. Male catchers must also wear a cup.

Each member of the team has a number on the back of his or her uniform.

The different gloves from left to right: outfield, catcher's, infield, first base

The catcher is well-protected from fast pitches and foul tips.

The baseball glove

Each player on the fielding team wears a glove on his or her non-throwing hand to catch and field with. The best gloves are made of leather, are lightweight, and well padded.

There are different gloves for different kinds of fielding.

- The first base fielder wears a large glove with extra webbing to trap balls.

- The catcher uses a large rounded glove with more padding because he or she must catch pitches that are often thrown at high speeds.

- The infield glove is worn by the second and third base players, shortstop, and the pitcher. An infielder's glove is smaller to make it easier to field ground balls and to quickly grab the ball to throw.

- The outfield glove is large to help catch fly balls.

Selecting a glove

When selecting a glove, choose one that is comfortable. The correct size will ensure comfort and control.

Caring for a new glove

A new glove needs to be shaped. To make a good pocket for catching, catch a ball in it as often as you can. When not in use, work some glove oil into the palm area of the glove and put a baseball into it so that it takes the shape of the ball. From time to time, rub some oil into your glove to keep it soft.

Baseball 11

What You Need to Play

The baseball bat

In youth leagues, bats are usually made of aluminum or other metal materials. Professional leagues allow the use of wood bats only. Aluminum bats are more durable and, though lighter, provide better hitting power than wooden bats. The hitting distance is about 10 per cent greater for aluminum bats.

The ideal bat for a 10–14-year-old player is 27–31 inches (70–80 cm) long, weighing 22–26 ounces (650–760 grams). Coaches recommend a bat which is light rather than heavy. This will provide better control and quicker bat speed.

The baseball

The baseball is made from yarn wound around a core of cork and rubber and covered with leather. Stitched seams hold the leather cover in place. The baseball has a circumference of 9–9.25 inches (22.8–23.4 cm) and a weight of 5–5.25 ounces (141.7–148.8 grams).

Younger players can play with a softer ball, such as a rubber-coated ball.

The bat needs to be light enough to swing quickly, but heavy enough to add power.

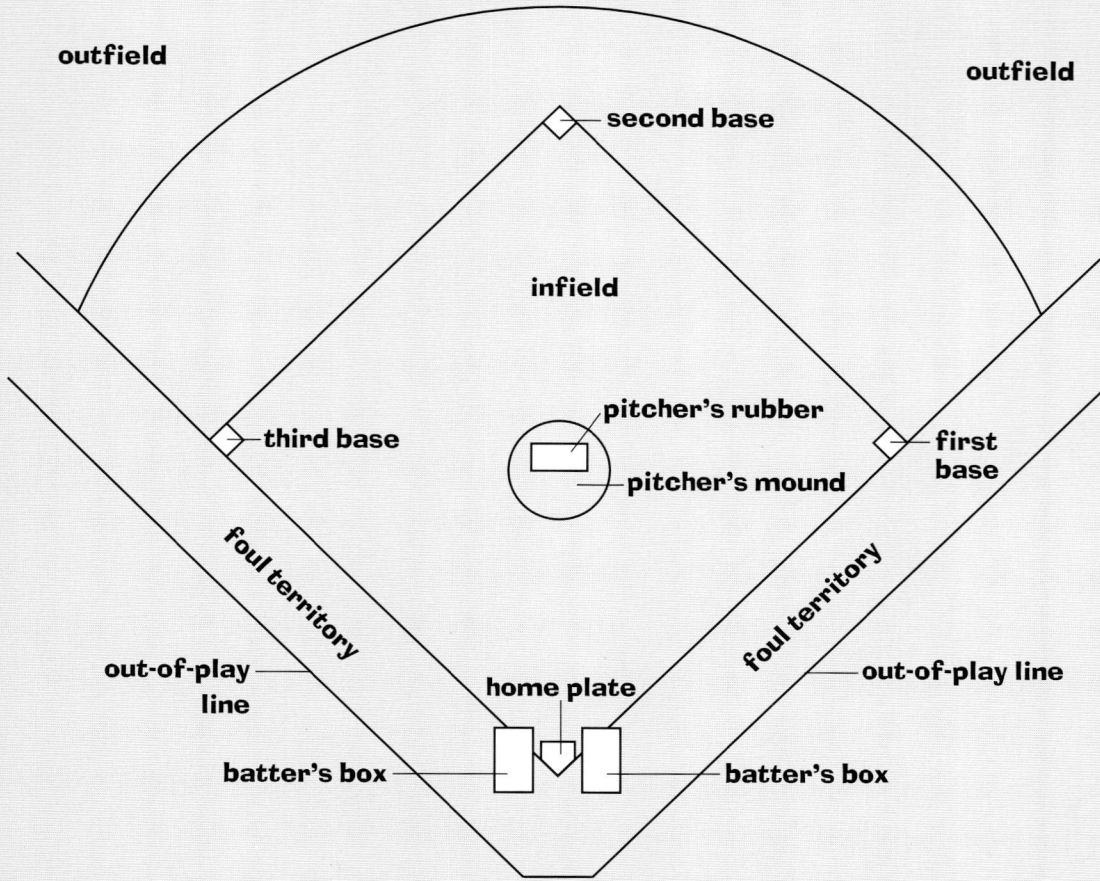

The baseball field

Play takes place on a field that consists of an **infield** and an **outfield**.

The infield

The infield, or **diamond**, is the area bounded by the bases. Distances around the diamond are:

- pitcher to home plate: 60 ft 6in. (18m)
- Base to base – 90 ft (27 m)

Juniors play on smaller diamonds.

At each corner of the diamond is a **base**. It is made of rubber-covered foam and staked to the ground. The **pitcher's rubber** is located in the center of the diamond on top of the **pitcher's mound.** Home plate is a solid piece of white rubber outlined in black.

When the ball passes over the line known as the **out-of-play line**, play stops. Runners are awarded an extra base. Play resumes with the pitcher pitching to the batter.

The outfield

The area beyond the infield and within the foul lines, is the outfield. Three fielders are positioned in the outfield to field any balls that are hit past the infielders.

The entire infield and outfield area within the boundary lines is known as **fair territory**. **Foul territory** is the area outside of the boundary lines known as the foul lines. The batter must hit the ball into fair territory to be able to run to base safely.

Rules

Pitching

The pitcher stands on the **pitcher's mound,** which is in the center of the infield. He or she tries to throw the ball through the **strike zone**. When the ball goes through the strike zone, the umpire will call "**strike**," regardless of whether the batter has swung at the ball.

A pitched ball passes through the strike zone when it travels:

- directly above home plate
- higher than the batter's knees
- and lower than the batter's armpits.

If the pitcher's accuracy is poor and the ball is outside the hitter's strike zone, the umpire will call "**ball**." When four "balls" are pitched to one batter, the umpire will direct the batter to "take a walk." Even though the batter has not hit the ball, he or she goes to first base.

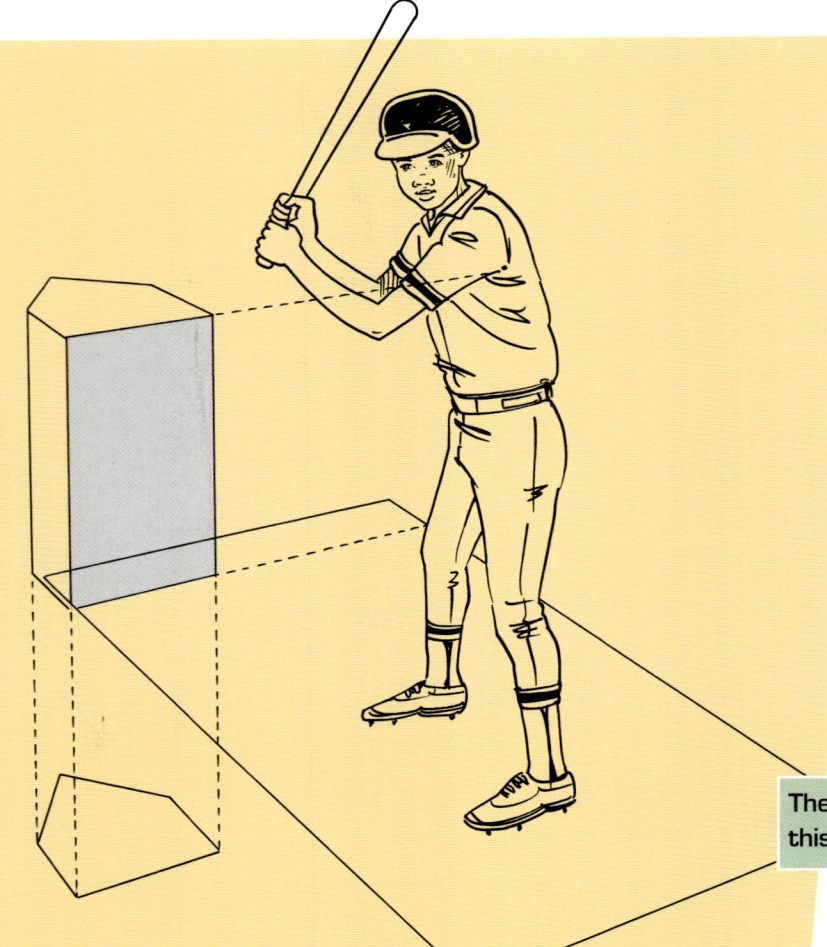

The shaded area shows this batter's strike zone.

Top Sport

Batting

The batter can choose to swing at any ball whether it is in the strike zone or not. The umpire will always call "strike" when the batter swings and misses, even if the ball is out of the strike zone.

When the batter hits the ball into **fair territory,** he or she must drop the bat and run to first base. If there is a **runner** on first base, the runner must leave this base and run to second base. Two players are not allowed to share one base.

When the batter hits the ball into **foul territory**, the umpire will call "**foul ball.**" The batter cannot run to first, nor is he or she out, unless the ball is caught. Fouls are counted as strikes. If the batter has two strikes, any further fouls are not counted as strikes unless they are caught or if the batter **bunts** foul, in which case it is strike three and the batter is out.

If the batter swings at the ball and misses, the umpire calls "strike."

Home Plate Umpire

The home plate umpire's duties include calling balls and strikes, score keeping, calling batters and runners out, and recording the use of substitute players.

The home plate umpire stands directly behind the catcher and leans forward for every pitch to judge whether it passes through the strike zone.

Baseball

Rules

Getting the batter out

The batter is out when he or she has unsuccessfully swung at three pitches. This is called a strike out. The umpire can can also call the batter out on strikes if he or she doesn't swing at pitches that go through the **strike zone.**

The batter is also out if he or she hits a ball that is caught, even if the ball is caught in **foul territory.**

Base running

When the batter hits the ball into **fair territory,** he or she must run to first base.

Base running

Only one **base runner** may be on a base at a time. Move to first, second, third, and home plate as quickly and safely as you can.

At first base, the batter may run through the base and still be safe as long as he or she touches the base before the first base fielder catches the ball. If the batter reaches the base before the ball, he or she is said to have made a single. Reaching second base is called a double, third base a triple, and if the the batter can make it around all four bases, he or she is said to have hit a **home run**. To score, a batter must make it safely to **home plate.** If he or she is out along the way, then no score is recorded.

If a batter has two strikes, then swings and misses the next pitch, he or she is out.

Stealing bases

Once on base, the batter is called a base runner. He or she may advance in several ways. Usually, the base runner will progress when the batter hits the ball. The runner can **steal** a base by running hard to the next base without the help of a hit. The pitcher and fielders always watch very closely for runners stealing bases. Fielders will then try to throw the runner out at the base to which the runner is going. The runner will often **slide** or dive to reach the base safely. Some youth leagues do not allow stealing.

Retiring the base runner

A runner who is touched with the ball while off base is **tagged out**. A runner is also out if he or she is beaten to the base by the ball. The runner is beaten to the base by the ball when the base fielder has possession of the ball and is touching the base.

Force play

A **force play** happens when a base runner is forced to move to the next base as an incoming runner is arriving. If the ball is thrown and caught at the next base before he or she arrives, the base runner is automatically out. For example, when a batter hits a fair ball and there is a runner on first base, that runner must advance to second base to allow the batter to run to first base. The runner is in a force play because he or she is forced to run to second base.

A force play is a good chance for the fielding team to try to get the ball to the base before the runner.

Fly ball rule

A ball hit high into the **outfield** is called a **fly ball.** A runner should run half way to the next base on a fly ball because if the ball is caught, he or she must return to the base. If the fielders get the ball to the base first before the runner, then the base runner is out. Runners advance on a fly ball only if they are sure it won't be caught.

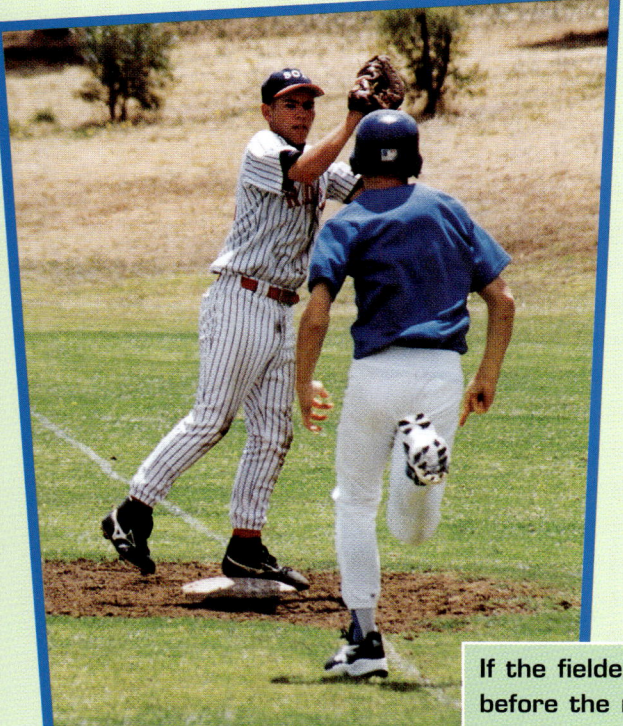

If the fielders get the ball to the base before the runner, the runner is out.

Skills

Batting

In most leagues, every member of the team has a turn to bat, so it is important to learn the skills of good batting. When you hit the ball, you are trying to hit it into **fair territory** so that it is difficult to field. This will give you and any **base runners** the best chance of scoring runs.

Gripping the bat

1. Hold the bat firmly with your fingers just above the bottom of the bat. Your hands should be close enough to touch one another.
2. To get the feel of the swing, hold the bat firmly, but not too tightly, and swing it freely several times.
3. If the bat feels too long or too heavy, get another one. Otherwise, move your hands farther up the bat. This is called *choking up* on the bat.

The batting stance

With your feet slightly wider than shoulder-width apart, stand with your body facing home plate. Extend your bat to touch the end on home plate.

Now raise the bat and bring it back so that your hands are at about shoulder height. Your weight is mostly on your rear foot at this stage in the swing.

Keep your hands relaxed. The tighter your grip, the less power you will have.

Hitting the ball

To begin the swing, take a small step with your front foot and point your toes at the pitcher. Coil your hips and shoulders. Extend your arms as you bring the bat to the ball. Keep your front leg straight, your chin tucked in to your chest, and your head still as you hit the ball.

Use a Tee-ball stand to practice your swing.

Swing the bat from behind your shoulders, keeping your eyes on the ball and the bat horizontal as you make contact with the ball.

Always try to swing the bat level with the ground or on a slightly downward angle. Bend or straighten your knees to adjust the height of your swing. For a low ball, bend your knees to get down to the ball. If you let the bat drop down, you probably will hit the ball into the air and it will be caught.

After contact, let your bat swing through freely. Remember that once you have hit the ball, you must run to first base.

Bunting

A **bunt** is a lightly hit ball that travels just a short distance into the **infield**. The bunt is useful in safely moving runners to the next base. From the normal batting stance, quickly slide the top hand to the middle of the bat and turn to face the pitcher.

A sacrifice bunt will move a runner safely to the next base by not allowing fielders to make a play on the runner. The batter purposely gives up his chance for a hit.

Baseball

Skills

Base running

After hitting the ball, the batter becomes a **base runner.** To score a run, he or she must advance around each of the bases and return to **home plate.**

Your first goal is to get safely to first base. Once you have hit the ball, drop your bat, turn fast, accelerate hard, and run as fast as you can to first base. You are allowed to overrun first base, so you must try to reach it before the ball reaches the first base player. At second and third base, you may not overrun the base. You must be on the base to be safe.

Advancing when on base

As the pitcher begins the **windup,** take your **lead off.** Slowly shuffle your feet while crouching and watching the pitcher. As the pitcher releases the ball, take several steps toward the next base. When the ball is hit, run quickly to the next base. Remember, you may also **steal** as soon as the ball leaves the pitcher's hand.

This runner reaches first base before the fielder receives the ball. He is safe!

20 Top Sport

When advancing from one base to the next, watch the fielders carefully to make sure they do not throw the ball to the base you are going to. There will be times when you will have to go back and times when you will be tagged out.

Sliding

The **slide** is often used by a base runner to avoid a **tag out** by sliding under a base fielder or to avoid injury through a collision. The most common and safest slide is the pop-up slide.

The pop-up slide

Extend your leading leg straight towards the base. Bend your other leg underneath.

As your foot makes contact with the base, push into an upright position.

Move quickly so that your back foot is on the base and you are ready to run to the next base.

Baseball 21

Skills

Pitching

The **pitch** begins the baseball game. The pitcher's main goal is to force the opposing team to make outs. He or she does this primarily by throwing strikes. This will force batters to swing at the pitches. When pitching, use a natural and comfortable throwing motion. Start with some easy throws to the catcher, concentrating on accuracy. Then increase the speed.

The pitching grip

In the **windup** delivery, stand facing the batter. Bring your hands forward and up with the ball in your glove. Raise the leg opposite your throwing arm and turn your body to the side. Keep your throwing elbow high and extend your arm back. Your shoulders and hips are now sideways to the batter.

Try to throw "through" the target. This will require a smooth windup motion, good arm extension, a strong push off with your legs, and a proper follow-through after releasing the ball.

The pitching grip

The seams on a baseball are used for grip. Place your index and middle fingers about an inch (2.5 cm) apart across the seams at the top of the ball, and your thumb and fourth finger underneath.

The pitching philosophy

The pitcher's goal is to make hitting as difficult as possible. This means throwing the ball fast and throwing **off-speed pitches**. Good pitchers throw to different locations in and out of the **strike zone** to try to get hitters to swing at bad pitches.

Variety of pitches

As your skills and body develop, so will your control of the ball. Experiment with different grips to change the flight and speed of the ball. This will confuse the batter. Young pitchers should avoid throwing curve balls that might damage their still-growing arms

Step towards the batter and release the ball as your front foot lands.

Follow through down and across your body. Now move quickly to be ready to protect your body and to field the ball.

Skills

Catching

The catcher is a very important player. He or she must possess excellent catching skills and a strong, accurate throwing arm. The catcher is usually the player who positions and instructs the other fielders because he or she can see the entire field.

The correct catching position is as close as possible to the batter without being in the line of the batter's swing. Squat low with your feet a little wider than shoulder-width apart. Hold your glove out so that it forms a target for the pitcher. Move the target around, depending on where you want the pitcher to throw.

Protect your throwing hand by resting it behind the glove. You can use this hand to help squeeze the glove once you catch the ball. As your catching and throwing skills improve, you may also hide your throwing hand behind your leg. This provides more protection from **foul balls,** but may slow down your throws.

If a **runner** tries to **steal** a base, your first responsibility is to catch the ball. Then quickly move your feet into throwing position.

The throw should reach the base fielder at about knee height on the side from which the base runner is coming. The runner will then slide into the fielder's glove and be **tagged out.**

Because catchers have to throw quickly, they must shorten the throwing motion. Bring the ball back slightly past your head and release the ball with a sharp "flicking" motion with your wrist.

Squat low and keep your weight on the balls of your feet. Be ready to move your feet and body to block pitches in the dirt.

24 Top Sport

Fielding

As a fielder, your ability to catch and throw quickly helps you to get a batter or runner out. Your goal is to catch or field the ball and then throw to your target in the least possible time. This will put pressure on the base runner or even throw him or her out. Be ready to field the ball on each pitch and think about what to do if the ball is hit to you. Know where the base runners are so you know where to throw the ball.

The fly ball

Watch the ball closely as it leaves the bat. Quickly judge the speed and direction of the ball and then move to where the ball will land. Run lightly on the balls of your feet so you can see the ball clearly. As the ball approaches, stand square to the ball with your glove-side foot slightly ahead, feet apart. With your eyes still watching the ball, bring your glove and throwing hand up to catch the ball. Make sure you do not block your view of the ball with your glove. Firmly squeeze the glove as the ball enters it. Use your throwing hand to cover and squeeze the glove as well.

The waist-high ball

A ball coming at waist height can be hard to catch. Move your glove hand so that your palm faces down. Keep your fingers parallel to the ground and your thumb down, but keep your throwing hand palm up. Watch the ball into the glove and use your throwing hand to keep it in there.

With your knees bent, stand ready to move in any direction to field the ball.

Keep the elbow of your glove hand up for catching the waist-high ball.

Baseball 25

Skills

The ground ball

Move quickly into the path of the ball. Stand with your hands hanging loosely and your body weight slightly forward on the balls of your feet. Keep your body square to the ball and your hands low to the ground by bending at the hips and knees.

As the ball approaches, keep your hands low and open your glove. Watch the ball as it enters your glove. Your throwing hand then smothers the ball in the glove.

Throwing the ball

Once you have gathered the ball, you must throw it to your target quickly and accurately. Bring the glove and throwing hand up toward your chest and then into the regular throwing position. Grip the ball with your fingers across the seams, and turn sideways to your target. Bring your throwing arm back, with the ball at ear-height.

Step towards your target, leading the arm movement with your elbow as you transfer your weight to your front foot. Keep your throwing elbow at about shoulder height. Flick your wrist as your throwing hand comes over your elbow to release the ball. Turn your hips square to your target as you follow through down and across your body.

Fielding backhand

When the ball approaches from your nonglove side, you may need to field backhand.

If possible, keep your body momentum moving forward as you field a ground ball. Don't let the ball "play" you.

Backhand groundball Move quickly to the ball. Your glove elbow faces the ball as you bend low.

Forehand groundball Bend at the knees and waist to lunge for the ball. Try to stay on your feet.

Getting Ready

For practice or competition, it is important to warm-up your body. Start with these stretches and exercises and then do some slow jogging. Repeat each one four to six times. This will help you to perform well and reduce the risk of injury.

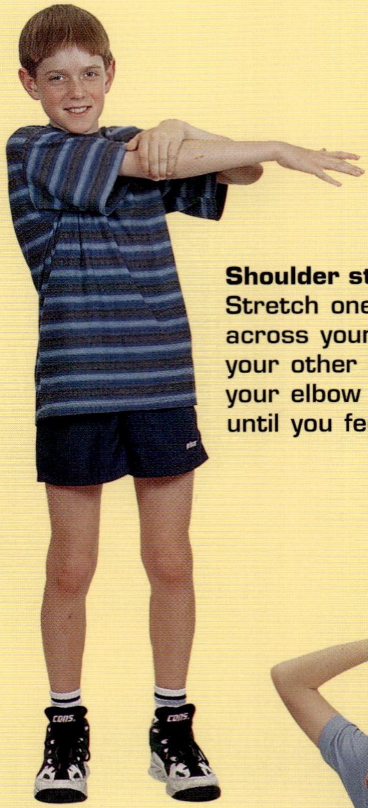

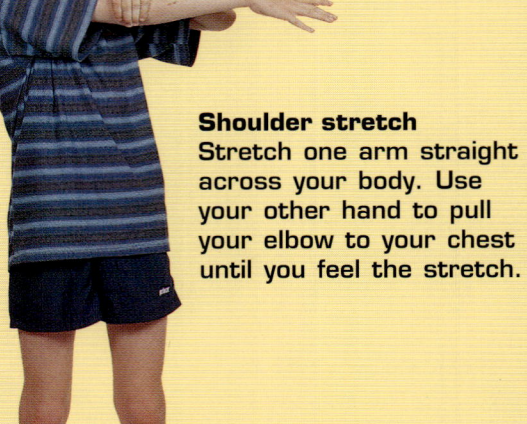

Shoulder stretch
Stretch one arm straight across your body. Use your other hand to pull your elbow to your chest until you feel the stretch.

Lower back stretch
Lie on your back with your legs outstretched. Bend one knee up to your chest and lift your head and shoulders off the floor to meet it. Lower yourself and then stretch the other side.

Arm and shoulder stretch
Bend your arm behind your head and gently push your elbow down with the other hand.

Treadmills
Put your hands on the ground, shoulder-width apart, with your legs stretched out behind you. Bring one foot forward and then replace it and bring the other foot up.

28 Top Sport

Arm circles
Stretch your arms above your head. Then take them around in circles forwards, then backwards. Stretch as far up and around as you can.

Calf stretch
Stand with one foot in front of the other. Bend your leading leg and lean forward, keeping both feet flat on the floor. Hold the stretch for about 10 seconds, then stretch the other leg.

Quadriceps stretch
Hold a partner with one hand for balance. Bend one knee and gently pull your foot up behind you. Hold the stretch for about 10 seconds and then stretch the other leg.

Star jumps
Stand with your feet together and your arms by your sides. Jump up and land with your feet apart and your arms outstretched. Then jump back to the start position.

Baseball 29

Taking It Further

American Amateur Baseball Congress (AABC)
118-19 Redfield Plaza, P.O. Box 467
Marshall, MI 49068
☎ (616) 781-2002

Continental Amateur Baseball Association (CABA)
82 University Street Westerville, OH 43081
☎ (614) 899-2103

Little League Baseball, Inc.
P.O. Box 3465 Williamsport, PA 17701
☎ (717) 326-1921

Pony Baseball, Inc
P.O. Box 225 Washington, PA 15301
☎ (412) 225-1060

United States Amateur Baseball Federation (USABF)
7355 Peter Pan Ave.
San Diego, Ca 92114
☎ (619) 527-9205

More Books to Read

Foster, Kelli C., and Gina C. Erickson. *Let's Play Ball*. Hauppauge, NY: Barron's Educational, 1996.

Geng, Don. *Fundamental Baseball*. Minneapolis, Minn: Lerner Publishing Group, 1995.

Santella, Andrew. *Baseball*. Crystal Lake, Ill: Rigby Interactive Library, 1996.

Shapiro, Ouisie, and Nancy Blumenthal. *Batter Up!: Baseball Activities for Kids of All Ages.* Reading, Mass: Addison-Wesley Educational Publishers, 1996.

Glossary

"ball" pitch that does not travel through the **strike zone**

base foam-filled square bag at each corner of the **diamond**

base runner player from the batting team who is either on a base or is running between bases

bunt lightly hit ball that travels a short distance, usually done to move **base runners**

diamond infield of the baseball field

fair territory area of the playing field between the first and third base foul lines and out to the playing boundaries

fly ball ball that is hit into the air

force play when a **base runner** is forced to advance a base because another base runner is running to his or her base

foul ball ball hit into **foul territory**

foul territory area outside the **diamond** and **outfield**

home run hit in which a batter reaches all four bases in one play, scoring a run

inning one turn at bat for each team

infield area within the diamond

lead off short, walking head start **runners** take on each **pitch**

offspeed pitch pitch that is purposely thrown slower to confuse a batter

out-of-play line line that marks the edge of the playing area

outfield area beyond the **infield** but within the boundary lines of the first and third base foul lines

pitch throwing of the ball from the pitcher to the batter

pitcher's mound raised circle of dirt from where the pitcher delivers **pitches**

pitcher's rubber strip of rubber from which the pitcher must push off to throw

slide when a **runner** leaves his or her feet in an attempt to reach a base without being tagged out

spikes shoes with metal or plastic points that provide traction

stealing to move from one base to another as a pitch is delivered to home plate

strike pitch that is not hit by the batter, and that travels through the strike zone

strike zone area above the home plate between the batter's knees and armpits

tagged out when a base runner is touched by the ball which is held by a fielder, while the runner is not on a base

tee ball type of baseball played by young players, in which batters hit the ball off a stand called a "tee"

windup motion that begins the pitcher's delivery to home plate

Baseball 31

Index

ball 12
base running 16, 20
bases 12
bat 12
batting 15, 18, 19
bunting 19

catcher 10–11, 24
Cartwright, Alexander J. 8
clothing 10–11

diamond 13
Doubleday, Abner 8

equipment 10–11

field 13
fielding positions 5
fielding 25, 26, 27
fly ball 17
force play 17
foul territory 13, 16

glove 11
grip
  batter 18
  pitcher 22–23

history 8–9
Holmes, Oliver Wendell 8
home run 7–8, 16

infield 12
innings 5

Maris, Roger 7, 8
McGwire, Mark 7, 8

Olympic Games 9
outfield 12

pitching 14, 22–23
players 12

ready position
  batter 18
  catching 24
  fielding 25, 26
  pitcher 22, 23
Ruth, Babe 7, 8

scoring 5
sliding 21
Sosa, Sammy 8
stealing base 17
strike 14, 15, 16
strike zone 14, 15

tagging 17
tee ball 5
throwing skills 26–27

umpire 15
uniform 10

World Series 9
warm-ups 28–29

DISCARDED BY
SAYVILLE LIBRARY

9/08

SAYVILLE LIBRARY
11 COLLINS AVE.
SAYVILLE, NY 11782